MONUMENTAL MONEY

People and Places on U.S. Paper Money

Yigal Arkin

MONUMENTAL MONEY

People and Places on U.S. Paper Money

Yigal Arkin

MONUMENTAL MONEY
People and Places on U.S. Paper Money

Research and text: Yigal Arkin
Editor: Lita Morgenstern Arkin
Graphics design: Lea Wilf
Cover design: Yigal Arkin

Published by **Arkin Publishing**
books@arkinnet.com

Library of Congress Control Number: 2011904400
ISBN 978-0-615-46454-1

CONTENTS

PART 1

THE FEDERAL RESERVE NOTES

PART 2

THE HISTORY OF THE AMERICAN MONETARY SYSTEM
A BRIEF REVIEW

PART 3

HIGH DENOMINATION NOTES

Did You Know... ?

PREFACE

This book is the culmination of many years of collecting banknotes. The idea to compile the book was sparked some years ago when I came across the 1976 two-dollar note issued to commemorate the Bicentennial of the United States of America.

I have always been interested in why certain people, places, events and symbols are selected to appear on banknotes. Some, of course, are obvious, such as George Washington and Abraham Lincoln. However many less obvious choices have also been made during the years. A large selection is illustrated here, together with a short explanation of the importance, meaning and historical relevance of each note.

I have aimed at producing a readable and interesting book, not overloaded with complicated professional terminology but accurate nonetheless. Hopefully you will discover or rediscover intriguing facts that will take you on a fascinating journey through time.

The book is divided into three parts.

PART 1   presents all the notes in circulation today, including those being slowly withdrawn from circulation as newer designs replace them. It includes color photographs and a brief description of the people and sites depicted on each banknote.

PART 2   presents a brief review of the history of the U.S. monetary system through the many types of banknotes in use from the time of the British Colonial Period (1690) to the present day.

PART 3   presents the high denomination notes that are no longer in circulation and that most people possibly never knew existed.

I hope you will enjoy thumbing through the book, reading the parts that interest you most and then going back to read the rest.

I would like to thank the following for their assistance: Elon Malis; Mira and Moshe Romano; The Federal Reserve Bank of San Francisco; Arthur L. Friedberg from The Coin & Currency Institute; Richard Doty from The Smithsonian Institution and Heritage Auctions for allowing me to use banknotes from their collections; Douglas Mudd from the American Numismatic Association, Sherwin Pomerantz and Bevie Katz for their advice, and the many others, too many to mention here, who helped me during the various stages of creating this book.

A special thank you to my parents Lita Morgenstern Arkin and Jack Arkin for their support.

Yigal Arkin

The Federal Reserve Notes
in Circulation

pages 15-20

pages 21-28

pages 29-34

pages 35-40

pages 41-46

pages 47-52

pages 53-58

Part 1

The Banknotes
in Circulation Today

Federal Reserve Notes

■

Banknotes with green captions are Federal Reserve Notes first issued in 1928, and issued with some changes until 1999. The $1 note was first issued in 1963, and the $2 note in 1976. Both are still in circulation today.

■

Banknotes with blue captions are redesigned Federal Reserve Notes. The $100 note was issued in 1996, the $50 note in 1997, the $20 note in 1998, and the $10 and $5 notes in 2000. They replaced the previous notes in circulation.

■

Banknotes with purple captions are redesigned colored Federal Reserve Notes. The $20 note was issued in 2003, the $50 note in 2004, the $10 note in 2006, and the $5 note in 2008. The colored version of the one-hundred dollar note is being printed and will be issued in the near future. These notes replaced those previously in circulation.

The Origin of Coins and Banknotes

In the distant past, trade was conducted by barter, that is the exchange of goods, usually food products but also services. This system brought about the introduction of precious metals, usually gold or silver, as an easier means of exchange. The goods were weighed against pieces of metal of standard weights. Coins evolved from this idea and they were also cast in other metals. Because coins were too heavy to carry around easily, merchants in China would leave their coins with a trustworthy person and the merchant was given a slip of paper recording how much money he had left with that person. When he produced this "promissory note" he could redeem his money. In the 7th century the notes, paper money, were used alongside the coins.

Banknotes were introduced in Europe in the 14th century and in North America in the 1690s. The use of fixed denominations and printed banknotes came into use in the 18th century.

With the gradual removal of precious metals from the monetary system, banknotes evolved to represent credit money or, if backed by the credit of a government, fiat money. "Fiat" is the Latin word for "Let it be done".

Today, all national currencies are fiat currencies, including the US dollar.

Coins and banknotes make up the cash forms of all modern monetary systems. Coins are usually used for lower value units and banknotes for the higher values. In many monetary systems, the highest value coin made for circulation is worth less than the lowest value note.

The term dollar derives from the German word *thaler*, the name given to coins first minted in 1519.

ONE DOLLAR

George Washington appears on the face of the note, and both sides of the Great Seal of the United States appear on the back of the note. This note is still in circulation today.

b. February 22, 1732

d. December 14, 1799

GEORGE WASHINGTON, first president of the United States of America, served from 1789 to 1797.

Before becoming president, he led America's Continental Army to victory over the British during the American Revolutionary War (1775-1783).

As president he established the norm that no president should serve more than two terms. In 1797, he retired to his Virginia plantation where he died on December 14, 1799, aged 67. He is buried at Mount Vernon, Virginia. George Washington was married to Martha Dandridge Custis. They had no children together.

He played a central role in the founding of the United States and is one of the founding fathers.

Throughout the country there are many monuments in his honor. Among the most impressive is that on Mount Rushmore, South Dakota, where sculptures of the heads of George Washington, Thomas Jefferson, Theodore Roosevelt and Abraham Lincoln are carved into the face of the mountain. It is a well-known American landmark.

Among the many statements attributed to Washington are:

"Associate yourself with men of good quality if you esteem your own reputation; for 'tis better to be alone than in bad company."

■

"When we assumed the Soldier, we did not lay aside the Citizen."

Face of a one-dollar note with the portrait of George Washington.
This design was introduced in 1963 and is still in circulation today.

The Great Seal
of the United States,
reverse (left)
obverse (right)

THE GREAT SEAL OF THE UNITED STATES

Elements in the Great Seal of the United States representing the 13 original colonies:

- 13 stars
- 13 stripes
- 13 arrows
- 13 letters in the motto
- 13 leaves on an olive branch
- 13 olives on the branch
- 13 brick levels of the pyramid

The Great Seal of the United States is depicted on the back of the one-dollar note.

The seal is used to authenticate documents issued by the United States Government after the President has signed them.

On July 4, 1776, the Continental Congress chose a committee to design a great seal. Six years and three committees later, the Continental Congress had still not agreed on a design. Finally the task was given to Charles Thomson, the secretary of the Congress, who merged elements from all three previous designs. Congress approved Thomson's combined design on June 20, 1782, and it was engraved onto brass cylinders about 2.25 inches in diameter.

On September 16, 1782, Thomson used this seal for the first time to validate George Washington's signature on a document that authorized him to negotiate an exchange of prisoners from the War of Independence with Britain.

Thomson had custody of the seal until the creation of a new American government in 1789, when he handed the seal over to Thomas Jefferson, then Secretary of State.

Back of a $1 note depicting both sides of the Great Seal of the United States of America. This design was first put on the back of the 1935, $1 Silver Certificate, and has appeared on the Federal Reserve Note since 1963.

All subsequent Secretaries of State have been responsible for applying the seal to appropriate the documents.

The first seal was replaced in 1841, as it was worn out, and since then there have been several re-engravings. One of the seals is on display in the National Archives in Washington, D.C.

OBVERSE OF THE SEAL

The main figure on the obverse of the seal is a bald eagle with outspread wings, grasping a bundle of thirteen arrows in its left claw and an olive branch with thirteen leaves and thirteen olives in its right claw. The arrows and olive branch symbolize war and peace respectively. The eagle's head is turned towards the olive branch, symbolizing a preference for peace. The Latin words **E PLURIBUS UNUM** - "OUT OF MANY, ONE" - appear on the ribbon in the eagle's beak. A glory, an emanation of light rays, with thirteen stars appears over its head. The shield on the eagle has seven white stripes and six red stripes, representing the thirteen original colonies.

REVERSE OF THE SEAL

An incomplete pyramid with thirteen layers of bricks appears on the reverse of the seal. The year 1776 is inscribed in Roman numerals on the base of the pyramid and the radiant Eye of Providence watches over from above. The rising sun represents the birth of the nation. Two mottos in Latin appear on this side: **ANNUIT CŒPTIS** signifying that the Eye of Providence approves our undertakings; the second, **NOVUS ORDO SECLORUM** is a quotation from Virgil usually translated as "NEW WORLD ORDER".

Did you know?

- Martha Washington is the only woman to appear on a United States banknote.

  She appeared on the face of the **One Silver Dollar** note of 1886. In 1896 the Treasury issued a new one silver dollar certificate, which was one of the three notes known as the **Educational Series**. On the back there is a portrait of Martha Washington alongside her husband George Washington.

- George Washington has appeared on several notes of different denominations.

  Among them are the $500 and the $1,000 notes of 1861; the $1 note of 1869; the $2 note of 1899 and the $20 note of 1905.

  George Washington also appeared on **Fractional Currency** and **Confederate Currency**

  Since 1923, his portrait is the only one to appear on the $1 note.

$1 Note, Large Size,
Silver Certificate, 1886.
Portrait of Martha Washington.

TWO DOLLARS

Thomas Jefferson appears on the face of the note, and Monticello, Thomas Jefferson's home, appears on the back of the note. It was issued between 1928-1976.

In 1976, a new design for the back of the note was introduced, depicting the "Committee of Five" presenting their work to Congress. This was to commemorate the Bicentennial of the Independence of the United States. This design is still in use today.

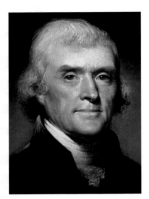

b. April 13, 1743
d. July 4, 1826

THOMAS JEFFERSON, the third President of the United States of America, served from 1801 to 1809. He was the first president to be inaugurated in Washington, D.C.

Thomas Jefferson was one of the principal authors of the Declaration of Independence of 1776. He served as the first United States Secretary of State from 1789-1793 and was one of the founders of the Jeffersonian Republican Party. He was also one of the founders of the University of Virginia. He promoted the separation of church and state.

Jefferson was a plantation owner, author, inventor, horticulturist, architect, archaeologist, paleontologist, and violinist. He was married to Martha Wayles Skelton and they had five children.

One of the well-known memorials in his honor is on Mount Rushmore in South Dakota, where a sculpture of his head is carved into the face of the mountain alongside sculptured portraits of three other presidents. Jefferson's head was first carved on George Washington's right. However after more than 18 months of work, it was deemed unsuccessful, dynamited off and carved again on Washington's left.

Two of Jefferson's controversial statements are:

"A little rebellion now and then is a good thing ..."

■

"When a man assumes a public trust, he should consider himself as public property."

Face of a two-dollar note with the portrait of Thomas Jefferson.
This design was issued from 1928.*

*This is a **United States Note (Legal Tender)** not a **Federal Reserve Note.** See explanation on p.75.

Face of a two-dollar note with the portrait of Thomas Jefferson.
This design was first issued in 1976 and is still in use today.

Monticello, Virginia, depicted on the back of the Two-Dollar **United States Note,** first issued in 1928.

MONTICELLO, located near Charlottesville, Virginia, was Thomas Jefferson's estate. Monticello, means "little mountain."

The construction of the building began in 1768 and was completed in 1809. The interior decoration of Monticello reflects the personal ideas and ideals of Jefferson.

- He incorporated a weather vane into the ceiling to show the direction of the wind.

- The large clock had only an hour hand since he thought this was accurate enough for outdoor laborers.

- The cloth floor was painted grass green, to bring the spirit of the outdoors into the house.

The building houses Jefferson's third library collection. His first library was burned down in a plantation fire. He sold his second library, his entire personal collection, to the Library of Congress to replace the books burned by the British during the War of 1812.

Jefferson considered furniture to be a waste of space, so the dining room table was put up only at mealtimes. Beds were built into alcoves cut into the thick walls. Alcoves were also used as storage space.

The house was in the center of a plantation of 5,000 acres, tended by some 600 slaves. Jefferson's eldest daughter, Martha, inherited the house but sold it in 1831. It changed hands several times until 1923, when it was purchased by the Thomas Jefferson Foundation, a private non-profit organization. Monticello is now a museum and educational institution.

Monticello was declared a World Heritage Site in 1987 and is the only home in the United States of America that has thus far been so designated.

Back of a two-dollar note depicting Monticello.
This design was first issued 1928.*

*This is a **United States Note (Legal Tender)** not a **Federal Reserve Note.** See explanation on p.75.

Committee of Five

The famous painting by John Trumbull, which hangs in the Rotunda of the United States Capitol, is usually incorrectly described as the Signing of the Declaration. What it actually shows is the Committee of Five presenting its work. Trumbull depicts most of the eventual signatories as being present on this occasion. However such a gathering never actually took place.

The 13 Colonies

- New Hampshire
- Massachusetts
- New York
- Rhode Island
- Connecticut
- New Jersey
- Pennsylvania
- Delaware
- Maryland
- Virginia
- North Carolina
- South Carolina
- Georgia

THE COMMITTEE OF FIVE. The Declaration of Independence is the document in which the thirteen colonies in North America declared their independent from Britain and explained their justification for so doing. It was ratified by the Second Continental Congress on July 4, 1776, in Philadelphia, Pennsylvania. This anniversary is celebrated as Independence Day in the United States of America.

In June 1776, a committee of five was formed to draft the declaration of this resolution including John Adams of Massachusetts, Benjamin Franklin of Pennsylvania, Thomas Jefferson of Virginia, Robert R. Livingston of New York and Roger Sherman of Connecticut. The Committee decided that Jefferson would write a draft and Franklin and Adams would make any necessary changes. The Committee finally presented the document to the Continental Congress on June 28, 1776 and independence was declared on July 2, 1776.

The full declaration was rewritten and adopted by the Continental Congress on July 4, 1776, at the Pennsylvania State House in Philadelphia and news of the declaration reached London on August 10, 1776.

After its adoption by Congress on July 4, a handwritten draft was sent to the printing shop of John Dunlap. Through the night between 150 and 200 copies were made; they are now known as "Dunlap broadsides." The original handwritten draft disappeared. On July 19, Congress ordered a new handwritten copy to be made for the delegates to sign. This copy is on display at the National Archives in Washington D.C. It is one of the United States of America's most important founding documents.

Most of the 13 delegates signed it on August 2, 1776, in the geographical order of their colonies from north to south. The remaining delegates signed later. As new states joined the Congress, their delegates were allowed to add their signatures. A total of 36 delegates eventually signed.

Back of a two-dollar note depicting the Committee of Five presenting its work to Congress. This change of design was made in 1976 to commemorate the Bicentennial of the Independence of the United States of America and it has appeared on all $2 notes since then.

DID YOU KNOW?

- Thomas Jefferson has appeared on several different denominations, including the $2 note shown below.

  Portraits of many others, such as Alexander Hamilton, William Windom, Secretary of the Treasury, and George Washington have also appeared on the $2 note. Since 1918, Thomas Jefferson is the only one to appear on this denomination.

  Thomas Jefferson also appeared on several different denominations of the **Fractional Currency.**

$2 Note, Large Size,
United States Notes, 1917.
Portrait of Thomas Jefferson.

FIVE DOLLARS

Abraham Lincoln appears on the face of the note, and the Lincoln Memorial appears on the back of the note. It was issued from 1928-2000.

In 2000, a new design replaced the previous notes.

The colored design was issued in 2008.

b. February 12, 1809
d. April 15, 1865

23 Union States:

- California
- Connecticut
- Delaware
- Illinois
- Indiana
- Iowa
- Kansas
- Kentucky
- Maine
- Maryland
- Massachusetts
- Michigan
- Minnesota
- Missouri
- New Hampshire
- New Jersey
- New York
- Ohio
- Oregon
- Pennsylvania
- Rhode Island
- Vermont
- Wisconsin

ABRAHAM LINCOLN, "Honest Abe", the sixteenth President of the United States, served from 1861 to 1865.

He was born in Kentucky. He served in the Illinois legislature and was later a judge.

When he became President he declared that the fate of the Union would rest in the hands of the South and that he would keep his oath **"to preserve, protect, and defend"** the Union. His election to the Presidency was one of the causes that prompted the American Civil War. Lincoln detested war, but when it came he accepted it as the only means of preserving the Union. Following the War, Lincoln viewed the ex-Confederate states as states that had tried to secede but had never left the Union.

Lincoln was shot twice by the actor John Wilkes Booth on Good Friday, April 14, 1865, while attending a performance at the Ford Theatre in Washington with his wife Mary and two guests. He died of his wounds the following day.

Among the many memorials in his honor, the two most impressive are the sculpture of his head carved into the face of Mount Rushmore, South Dakota and a seated sculpture of him in the Lincoln Memorial in Washington, D.C.

Lincoln is considered by many to have been the greatest president in United States history.

One of his famous statements is:

"You may fool all of the people some of the time; you can even fool some of the people all the time; but you can't fool all of the people all the time."

Face of a five-dollar note with the portrait of Abraham Lincoln.
This design was issued from 1928 to 2000.

Face of a five-dollar note with the portrait of Abraham Lincoln.
This design was introduced in 2000.

Face of a five-dollar note with the portrait of Abraham Lincoln.
This colored design was introduced in 2008.

The 36 States:

- Alabama
- Arkansas
- California
- Connecticut
- North Carolina
- South Carolina
- Delaware
- Florida
- Georgia
- Illinois
- Indiana
- Iowa
- Kansas
- Kentucky
- Louisiana
- Maine
- Maryland
- Massachusetts
- Michigan
- Minnesota
- Mississippi
- Missouri
- Nevada
- New Hampshire
- New York
- New Jersey
- Ohio
- Oregon
- Pennsylvania
- Rhode Island
- Tennessee
- Texas
- Vermont
- Virginia
- West Virginia
- Wisconsin

Lincoln Memorial, Washington D.C

The Lincoln Memorial in Washington D.C., depicted on the back of the five-dollar note, is a United States presidential memorial built in honor of President Abraham Lincoln.

The building is in the form of a Greek Doric temple and contains a large white marble sculpture of Lincoln seated gazing towards the Reflecting Pool and the Washington Monument. There are inscriptions carved into the walls from his second inaugural address and his Gettysburg address.

The site chosen in 1901 was originally swampland. The cornerstone was laid on February 12, 1914, Lincoln's birthday. The memorial was dedicated on May 30, 1922, attended by Lincoln's only surviving child, Robert Todd Lincoln.

The 36 massive columns incorporated into the structure represent the 36 States of the Union at the time of Lincoln's death in 1865. On the frieze above the colonnade are inscribed the names of the 36 states and the dates on which they entered the Union. Inscribed above the frieze are the names of the 48 states of the Union at the time of the dedication of the memorial. Alaska and Hawaii were added on a plaque at a later date.

Many famous speeches have been delivered on the front steps of the memorial, including Martin Luther King's "I Have a Dream" on August 28, 1963. A tile on the steps marks where Dr. King stood when he made his speech.

Back of a five-dollar note depicting the Lincoln Memorial.
This design was issued from 1928 to 2000.

Back of a five-dollar note depicting the Lincoln Memorial.
This design was introduced in 2000.

Back of a five-dollar note depicting the Lincoln Memorial.
This colored design was introduced in 2008.

DID YOU KNOW?

- Abraham Lincoln was the first president to be photographed at his inauguration, and the first president to be assassinated.

- Abraham Lincoln has appeared on several different denominations of dollar notes over the years.

  Among these notes were the $10 note of 1862, the $20 and $500 notes of 1863 and the $100 note which appeared later.

  He first appeared on the $5 note in 1914 and since then he is the only one to appear on this denomination.

  Abraham Lincoln also appeared on **Fractional Currency**.

$100 Note, Large Size,
United States Note, 1880.
Portrait of Abraham Lincoln.

TEN DOLLARS

Alexander Hamilton appears on the face of the note, and a view from the northwest of the U.S. Treasury building appears on the back of the note. It was issued from 1928-2000.

The note was redesigned in 2000 and the back of the new note shows the façade of the Treasury Building.

The colored design was issued in 2006.

b. January 11, 1755
or 1757

d. July 12, 1804

ALEXANDER HAMILTON, First Secretary of the Treasury, served from 1789 and 1795.

He was born on the West Indian island of Nevis on January 11, 1755, although he claimed 1757 as his birth year, the year when he first came to North America. In 1784, he founded the Bank of New York, the oldest banking organization still in existence in the United States.

Hamilton helped found the United States Mint, the First National Bank and the system of duties, tariffs, and taxes. In 1790, he established the U.S. Coast Guard under the auspices of the Department of the Treasury. In 1795, he resigned from the Treasury and went on to practice law, opening his own law office in New York City. He founded the Federalist Party which he headed until 1800.

Alexander Hamilton's life ended as a result of a duel with Vice President Aaron Burr that took place on July 11, 1804, on the banks of the Hudson River, New Jersey. The duel began at dawn. Hamilton's shot broke a tree branch directly above Burr's head. Burr's shot hit Hamilton who died the following day and was buried in the Trinity Churchyard Cemetery in Manhattan. A statue of Hamilton stands on the south side of the Treasury building in Washington, D.C. His Upper Manhattan home is preserved as the Hamilton Grange National Memorial.

**Two of the many statements attributed
to Hamilton are:**

*"I never expect to see a perfect work from
an imperfect man."*

■

*"Those who stand for nothing fall
for anything."*

Face of a ten-dollar note with the portrait of Alexander Hamilton.
This design was issued from 1928 to 2000.

Face of a ten-dollar note with the portrait of Alexander Hamilton.
This design was introduced in 2000.

Face of a ten-dollar note with the portrait of Alexander Hamilton.
This colored design was introduced in 2006.

The U.S. Treasury Building,
viewed from the northwest. A similar view of the building appeared on the back of the
$10 note printed between 1928 and 1999. In 1999 the note was redesigned and a front
view of the Treasury building is now shown on the back of this note.

The U.S. Treasury building is located on Capitol Hill, Washington D.C. on the southeast side of the White House. It is primarily used as the executive office of the Secretary of the Treasury and his deputy.

The building was destroyed by fire several times; in 1801, in 1814, during the war against the British, and in 1833, by arsonists. Only the fireproof wing was left standing.

There are 15 vaults of different sizes in the basement. At one time these vaults held currency, bonds, securities, gold and silver bullion.

There are 34 pillars on the east side of the building facing Fifteenth Street, 18 pillars on the west side, 10 on the north side and 10 on the south side, 72 pillars in all.

A statue of Alexander Hamilton, first Secretary of the Treasury, stands on the south patio of the building.

Back of a ten-dollar note depicting the U.S. Treasury building from the northwest. This design was issued from 1928 to 2000.

Back of a ten-dollar note depicting the front of the U.S. Treasury building. This design was introduced in 2000.

Back of a ten-dollar note depicting the front of the U.S. Treasury building. This colored design was introduced in 2006.

DID YOU KNOW?

- Alexander Hamilton has appeared on several different denominations of U.S. banknotes.

  He first appeared on the 1861, $5 **Demand Note** which some consider to be the first U.S. note put into circulation.

  He then appeared on the $2 note shown below, the $5, $20 and $50 **Legal Tender Notes** of 1862 to 1869 and on the $50 and $500 **Interest Notes** issued at the same time.

  In 1918, he appeared on the $1,000 note. The first time he appeared on the $10 note was in 1928. Since then he is the only one to appear on this denomination

- Portraits of presidents and other eminent figures that appear on banknotes are usually similar, or with only very minor differences, even when they appear on different banknotes. Alexander Hamilton was an exception. Four significantly different portraits of him have appeared over the years on different denominations.

  He is also the only person to have appeared simultaneously on four denominations of the same series of notes - the **Legal Tender** series. The $2, $20 and $50 notes use the same portrait; the $5 note uses a different portrait.

$2 Note, Large Size, United States Note, 1862. Portrait of Alexander Hamilton.

TWENTY DOLLARS

Andrew Jackson appears on the face of the note, and the south side of the White House appears on the back of the note. It was issued from 1928-1934.

The back of the note was redesigned in 1934 and from then till 1998 the note was printed with a view of the remodeled south side of the White House.

In 1998 the note was again redesigned and the north side of the White House appears on the back of the note.

The colored design was issued in 2003.

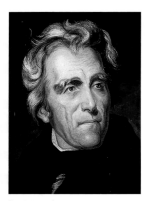

b. March 15, 1767

d. June 8, 1845

ANDREW JACKSON, seventh President of the United States, served from 1829 to 1837.

At the age of thirteen he joined the Continental Army as a courier. He was captured and imprisoned by the British during the American Revolutionary War.

Before his election to the presidency, he was the first governor of Florida (1821).

On January 30, 1835, an unsuccessful attempt was made to assassinate him.

Andrew Jackson was the last U.S. President to have been a veteran of the American Revolutionary War and the only president to have been a prisoner of war.

In 1837, he retired to Nashville and enjoyed eight years of retirement. He died on June 8, 1845, at the age of 78.

Memorials to Jackson include three identical statues: one in Jackson Square, New Orleans, Louisiana; one in the Nashville Tennessee State Capitol and one in Washington D.C., near the White House.

A statue of Jackson also stands in the Capitol rotunda in front of the doorway in which the assassination attempt of 1835 took place.

One of the many statements attributed to Jackson is:

*"One man with courage makes
a majority."*

Face of a twenty-dollar note with the portrait of Andrew Jackson.
This design was issued from 1928 to 1998.

Face of a twenty-dollar note with the portrait of Andrew Jackson.
This design was introduced in 1998.

Face of a twenty-dollar note with the portrait of Andrew Jackson.
This colored design was introduced in 2003.

The White House - north façade   **The White House** – south façade

THE WHITE HOUSE, which appears on the back of the $20 note, is the official home and principal workplace of the President of the United States of America. It is located at 1600 Pennsylvania Avenue NW, in Washington D.C.

Its construction began with the laying of the cornerstone on October 13, 1792. It was built of sandstone, painted white and was completed on November 1, 1800. John Adams was the first president to take up residence in the building.

It has been reconstructed several times. In 1814, during the War of 1812, it was burned down by the British Army, but rebuilt almost immediately. President James Monroe moved into the partially-reconstructed house in October 1817. It has been expanded and extended over the years to include a west wing and an east wing, executive offices, reception areas and living quarters. Jacqueline Kennedy, wife of President John F. Kennedy, 1961-1963, directed an extensive redecoration of the house during her husband's presidency.

It was originally referred to as the *President's Palace*, the *President's Mansion* or the *President's House*. The earliest evidence of the public calling it The *White House* was in 1811 and related to its white-painted exterior. In 1901, it was unofficially named by President Theodore Roosevelt as *White House-Washington*. President Franklin Roosevelt changed it to *The White House* with the word *Washington* beneath it, as it appears today.

Back of a twenty-dollar note depicting the south side of the remodeled White House. This design was issued from 1934 to 1998.

Back of a twenty-dollar note depicting the north side of The White House. This design was introduced in 1998.

Back of a twenty-dollar note depicting the north side of The White House. This colored design was introduced in 2003.

DID YOU KNOW?

- The first assassination attempt on a U.S. president was made on Andrew Jackson.

  On January 30, 1835, Richard Lawrence approached Jackson as he was leaving the United States Capitol building and aimed two pistols at him, both of which misfired.

- Andrew Jackson has appeared on several different denominations of U.S. banknotes.

  He first appeared in 1861 on the $50 note; in 1863 he appeared on the $10,000 note; in 1869 on the $5 note, and in 1918 on the $10 note.

  In 1928 he appeared on the $20 note and since then he is the only one to appear on this denomination.

  Andrew Jackson also appeared on **Confederate Currency.**

Back of a $20 note depicting a view of the south side of The White House before its remodeling. This was the design used from 1928 to 1934.

FIFTY DOLLARS

Ulysses S. Grant appears on the face of the note, and the east façade of the United States Capitol in Washington appears on the back of note. This note was issued between 1928-1997.

In 1997 the note was redesigned showing the west façade of the United States Capitol in Washington D.C. on the back of the note.

The colored design was issued in 2004.

b. April 27, 1822
d. July 23, 1885

ULYSSES SIMPSON GRANT, eighteenth President of the United States, served from 1869 to 1877.

He graduated from West Point Military Academy in 1843. A commanding general of the United States Army from 1864 to 1865, he led the victory over the Confederate Army led by Robert E. Lee. In April 1865. The Union Army captured Richmond, the Confederate capital. Lee surrendered to Grant and the Confederacy collapsed, thus ending the Civil War.

Enormously popular after the Union's victory, he was elected to the presidency in 1868, though he was politically inexperienced when he entered The White House.

He supported amnesty for Confederate leaders, the protection of civil rights of African Americans, and the suppression of the violent acts of the Ku Klux Klan.

Grant also signed a law that created Yellowstone National Park, America's first national park. He died on Thursday, July 23, 1885 at the age of 63 and was buried beside his wife in New York City's Riverside Park.

There are several monuments in his honor across the country, among them the Ulysses S. Grant Memorial located on Capitol Hill in Washington D.C. and a statue of Grant on Mount Cincinnati in Vicksburg, Mississippi.

One of the many statements attributed to Grant is:

*"Labor disgraces no man;
unfortunately, you occasionally find
men who disgrace labor."*

Face of a fifty-dollar note with the portrait of Ulysses S. Grant.
This design was issued from 1928 to 1997.

Face of a fifty-dollar note with the portrait of Ulysses S. Grant.
This design was introduced in 1997.

Face of a fifty-dollar note with the portrait of Ulysses S. Grant.
This colored design was introduced in 2004.

The United States Capitol.
This is a view of the west façade of the building as it appears on the back of the $50 note printed from 1996. The east façade was depicted on the the the back of the $50 note printed from 1928 to 1996.

THE UNITED STATES CAPITOL BUILDING, serves the Congress of the United States, the legislature of the U.S. Federal Government. It is located on Capitol Hill, Washington D.C. The building has a large dome above its rotunda and two wings. The chamber of the Senate is in the north wing and the chamber of the House of Representatives is in the south wing.

The current building is the fifth to serve the U.S. Federal Government. Its construction began in 1793 and George Washington laid the cornerstone. The U.S. Congress held its first session in the Capitol on November 17, 1800. Not long after its completion, the building was partially burned down by the British during the War of 1812. Reconstruction began in 1815 and was completed in 1830. It was expanded in the 1850s and the original timber-framed dome was replaced by a cast iron dome.

The east sector of the Capitol was rebuilt in 1904. Underground tunnels and an electric subway connects the main Capitol building with each of the congressional office buildings in the surrounding complex.

The building is open to visitors most days of the year and guided tours are available.

Back of a fifty-dollar note depicting the east side of the U.S. Capitol.
This design was issued from 1928 to 1997.

Back of a fifty-dollar note depicting the west side of the U.S. Capitol.
This design was introduced in 1997.

Back of a fifty-dollar note depicting the west side of the U.S. Capitol.
This colored design was introduced in 2004.

DID YOU KNOW?

- Ulysses S. Grant was elected President of the U.S. at the age of 46 and was the youngest person to be elected to this office until John F. Kennedy in 1960, at the age of 43.

- Ulysses Grant has appeared on several different denominations of U.S. banknotes.

  In 1886, he appeared on the **Five Silver Dollars Certificate**, shown below. In 1913, he appeared on the $50 note and since then he is the only one to appear on this denomination.

$5 Note, Large Size,
Silver Certificate, 1886.
Portrait of Ulysses Grant.

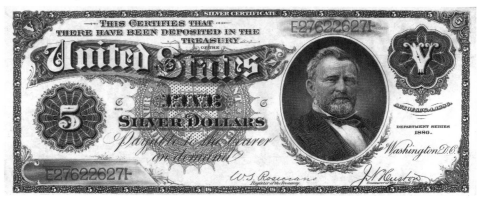

ONE HUNDRED DOLLARS

Benjamin Franklin appears on the face of the note, and Independence Hall, Philadelphia, appears on the back of the note.

In 1996 the note was redesigned and replaced the previous notes.

As part of the decision to issue colored versions of all the banknotes in circulation, with the exception of the $1 and $2 notes, the color version of the hundred dollar note is being printed and will be issued in the near future.

b. January 17, 1706
d. April 17, 1790

Franklin invented

- the lightning rod
- bifocal eye glasses
- the odometer
- the Franklin stove
- daylight saving time

BENJAMIN FRANKLIN was one of the founding fathers of the United States. Born in Boston, Massachusetts, he was the fifteenth child of twenty and the youngest son. He spent many years in England.

He was a newspaper editor, printer and merchant in Philadelphia and became very wealthy. By 1730, Franklin had set up a printing house of his own and published The Pennsylvania Gazette. Franklin was a Freemason and became a Grandmaster in 1734.

In 1776, he was a member of the Committee of Five that drafted the Declaration of Independence. He is the only founding father who signed all four of the major documents of the founding of the United States: the Declaration of Independence, the Treaty of Paris, the Treaty of Alliance with France and the United States Constitution.

He printed currency for the State of New Jersey based on an innovative anti-counterfeiting technique which he devised. From 1785, to his death he was President of the Supreme Executive Council of Pennsylvania. Towards the end of his life he was one of the most prominent supporters of abolition.

Benjamin Franklin died on April 17, 1790, at the age of 84. He is buried in Philadelphia, Pennsylvania.

Three of the many statements attributed to Franklin are:

"By failing to prepare, you are preparing to fail."

■

"Tell me and I forget. Teach me and I remember. Involve me and I learn."

■

"A man wrapped up in himself makes a very small bundle."

Face of a one-hundred dollar note with the portrait of Benjamin Franklin.
This design was printed from 1928 to 1996.

Face of a one-hundred dollar note with the portrait of Benjamin Franklin.
This design was introduced in 1996.

Face of a one-hundred dollar note with the portrait of Benjamin Franklin.
This colored design will be issued in the near future.

Independence Hall, Philadelphia, Pennsylvania

INDEPENDENCE HALL, which appears on the back of the $100 note, is officially known as the Pennsylvania State House. It is a national landmark located in Philadelphia, Pennsylvania. It was designed in the Georgian style and built between 1732-1753. The building is now part of the larger Independence National Historical Park and is listed as a World Heritage Site.

Originally built and used by the Colonial Government of Pennsylvania as its State House, it later served as the principal meeting place of the Second Continental Congress from 1775 to 1783. The Declaration of Independence was approved here on July 4, 1776, although the vote had actually taken place two days earlier, and was read out in the area now known as Independence Square.

The United States Constitution was drafted and signed here in 1787. The bell tower was the original home of the Liberty Bell. Today it holds a bell created for the United States Centennial Exposition in 1876. The original Liberty Bell with its distinctive crack is on display across the street in the Liberty Bell Center.

Back of a one-hundred dollar note depicting Independence Hall.
This design was printed from 1928 to 1996.

Back of a one-hundred dollar note depicting Independence Hall.
This design was introduced in 1996.

Back of a one-hundred dollar note depicting Independence Hall.
This colored design will be issued in the near future.

Did you know?

- Benjamin Franklin established the first fire department in the U.S. and funded the first lending library, which opened in Philadelphia.

- Benjamin Franklin has appeared on several different denominations of U.S. banknotes.

  He first appeared on the $50 note of 1874. He then appeared on the $10 note of 1879 and on the $100 note in 1914. Since then he is the only one to appear on this denomination.

  All the notes on which Benjamin Franklin appears carry a front face portrait with the exception of the 1914, $100 Federal Reserve Note, that shows Benjamin Franklin in profile, as shown below.

  He also appeared on **Fractional Currency.**

$100 Note, Large Size
Federal Reserve Note, 1914.
Portrait of Benjamin Franklin.

Part 2

The History of the American Monetary System

A Brief Review

DID YOU KNOW?

STAR NOTES

A Star Note is a banknote in which the serial number has a star printed either before or after it in place of a letter. A Star Note is a substitute note and replaces a defective note.

After printing and cutting, all banknotes of all types are packed in groups of one hundred with the serial numbers running in sequence. If during its manufacture a note with the serial number on it is found to be damaged or unfit for use, it has to be destroyed and replaced by another.

Replacing a particular note with its exact serial number is a complicated procedure and so the Star Note system was devised whereby a separate series of banknotes is printed with a serial number and a star alongside it.

Star Notes are printed in all denominations, but they are very rare, so if you come across one, hang onto it!

$100 Star Note,
Federal Reserve Note.
Portrait of Benjamin Franklin.

UNITED STATES HISTORY

HIGHLIGHTS OF EVENTS FROM 1492-1913

1492   **Christopher Columbus** and others discover America

1562   **First French colony:** Parris Island - off the coast of South Carolina

1585   **First English colony:** Roanoke Island – off the coast of North Carolina

1607   **First permanent English settlement in** the New World – on the coast of Virginia

1609   **Spaniards** settle Santa Fe, New Mexico

1620   The **Mayflower** arrives at Cape Cod on November 19

1624   **First Dutch colonies** in Albany and the Manhattan areas of New York

1640   **First book printed in America**

1676   Indian war

1683   **First German colony** – near Philadelphia

1731   **First circulating library** – founded in Philadelphia by **Benjamin Franklin**

1752   Liberty Bell delivered to Pennsylvania

1754   French-Indian War

1770   The Boston Massacre

1773   The Boston Tea Party

1774   **First Continental Congress**

1775   **George Washington** appointed Commander in Chief by the Continental Congress

1776   Declaration of Independence

1781   First commercial bank established

1789	**George Washington** appointed president by the Continental Congress
1791	**First Bank of the United States** charted by the Federal Government
1792	White House cornerstone laid on October 13
1800	Federal Government moved to Washington, D.C
1803	**Meriwether Lewis** and **William Clark** explore the Northwest U.S.
1812	War of 1812 – the United States versus the British
1835	Liberty Bell cracked
1846	Mexican War
1847	**First adhesive U.S. postage stamps: Franklin** – 5 cents; **Washington** – 10 cents
1849	The beginning of the California gold rush
1860	**First Pony Express**
1861	Civil War (1861-1865)
1863	**Abraham Lincoln** – Gettysburg Address
1867	Alaska bought by the U.S. from Russia for $7.2 million
1869	Black Friday attempt to corner gold
1872	First national park established – Yellowstone
1876	**Alexander Graham** Bell patented the telephone
1892	Ellis Island in New York Harbor opened to receive immigrants
1903	**First section** of the New York subway system opened
1913	**Federal Reserve banking system established**

THE AMERICAN MONETARY SYSTEM

The United States currency system seems simple but it is actually very complicated and cumbersome.

It is commonly accepted that in 1492 Christopher Columbus discovered the land known today as the North American continent. Soon after the discovery, England claimed the continent for itself, then Spain and France claimed territories. In the late 16th century, British, Spanish, French, and other European states began to colonize North America.

The ongoing tension between Britain and its 13 colonies in North America peaked in 1774. In 1776, they declared their independence from the British. Subsequently the American War of Independence began. It ended in 1783. After the early national period of 1783-1815 and the continental expansions of 1816-1860, came the Civil War of 1861-1865, which split the United States, by then 36 states, into two – the North and the South. They fought against each other for several years.

In 1865, at the end of the Civil War, the 36 states re-united to reconstitute the United States of America. In the years to follow other territories joined. Alaska and Hawaii were the last to join.

The 13 colonies that were under British rule were the first to issue paper money - paper money, not banknotes. The system of banks and their ability to issue notes was yet to be created. Because the 13 colonies were in fact the initiators of the United States, their colonial currency is considered to be a part of the history of American currency.

The Civil War of 1861-1865 created two governments: the Union Government (the United States Government) and the Confederate Government. The Confederates were the 11 states that had broken away from the Union of 36 states following Abraham Lincoln's election as president. Each government created its own currency: the Confederate Government created the **Confederate Currency** and the Union Government created the **United States Currency.** By the end of the Civil War, the **Confederate Currency** was worthless. After the reunion only the **United States Currency** was in use.

The financial crisis during the Civil War years forced the government of the Union States to issue several types of notes simultaneously. There were **Demand Notes, Treasury Notes,**

Interest Bearing Notes, Legal Tender Notes, Fractional Currency and **National Currency,** all in circulation at the same time. It was these many types of currency that led to the lack of trust in the currency system. It was not until 1913, that Congress realized that there was a dire need to create a more stable and unified system.

Subsequently the Federal Reserve Bank system was created, the currency notes were redesigned and from 1914 all notes were issued only by the Federal Reserve Bank, though there were still several types of currency issued simultaneously. There were **Gold Certificates, Silver Certificates, National Currency, Federal Reserve Bank Notes** and **Federal Reserve Notes.**

The currency was finally standardized in the mid-20th century. It is known as **Federal Reserve Notes** and is the currency in use today, though it has been redesigned many times over the years.

The paper money issued is commonly divided into 13 categories. Most were printed as **Large Size Notes** and **Small Size Notes**.

Large Size Notes were issued before 1928 and were printed on Large Size paper, approximately 7.5 by 3 inches (189 by 79 mm).

The first **Interest Bearing Notes** and the **Fractional Currency** issued between 1863-1876 were printed on much smaller paper and each denomination was a different size.

Small Size Notes are all the notes issued from 1928 onwards. The size of the paper was reduced to 6.14 by 2.61 inches (156 by 66 mm) and is the size still in use today.

In the following pages all 13 categories are presented clearly, each with a colored illustration of one or more of the notes of its issue, followed by a brief explanation.

I have avoided going into all the minor details that appear on the notes. For example, the date printed on the note is not necessarily the year the note was actually printed but rather the first year it was issued, or the year the signatories on the notes were changed. Nor have I gone into the rules of the **obligation to pay,** that is, the ability to redeem the notes in gold or silver, which were frequently changed.

Today's currency cannot be redeemed in gold or silver and is referred to as **Fiat Money**.

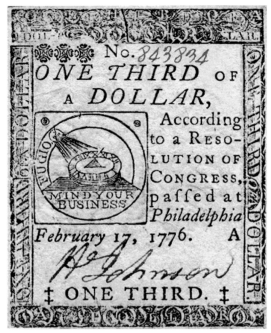

One third of a dollar, Continental Note, Philadelphia.

COLONIAL AND CONTINENTAL CURRENCY
1690-1788

Colonial **Currency** refers to the currency issued by the British colonies in the North American. They were issued as early as 1690, by colonies such as Massachusetts and New York, which issued notes in denominations of 5, 10, 20 shillings and 5 pounds. Other colonies issued notes in denominations of shillings and pounds and some in values of pennyweights, grains or ounces.

From 1775 the Continental Congress – the Congress of the 13 British colonies – created the **Continental Currency** that was isuued at the same time as the colonies issued their own paper money. These were in dollars or cents. They were issued until late 1789.

Colonial and **Continental** currencies were printed in hundreds of different varieties. None of these notes resemble the notes or paper money to which we are accustomed today.

$100 Treasury Note of 1865 with 5 coupons attached. Portrait of Winfield Scott.
This is a 3-year Interest Bearing Note giving two cents interest per day, that is, 7.3% per annum. The interest was redeemable by turning in the coupons attached to the Notes on the designated date which appeared on each coupon. The last six months of interest was redeemable only when the Note was turned in.

INTEREST BEARING NOTES 1812-1907

Four types of Interest Bearing Notes were issued over the years.

A
Treasury Notes of the War of 1812

B
Compound Interest Treasury Notes

C
Civil War Interest Bearing Notes

D
Refunding Certificates

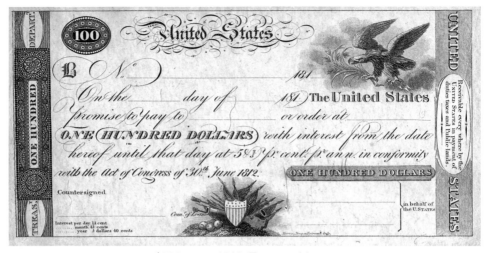

$100 note, 1812. Treasury Notes.

TREASURY NOTES

Treasury Notes of the War of 1812 were the first to be issued by the United States Congress. They were issued from 1812-1815 and were a type of loan certificate not initially intended for circulation. They were issued in various combinations from $20 to $100. All the notes depicted an eagle on the face and bore 5.4% interest per annum. Some of these notes were in fact in circulation and therefore were the first paper money notes of the U.S.

In 1815, the U.S. Treasury issued what are known as the Small Treasury Notes in denominations of $3, $5, $10, $20 and $50 which bore no interest and a $100 note which carried 5.4% interest. These, too, depicted variations of an eagle on the face.

In 1837, the U.S. Treasury issued new notes that carried interest rates ranging from 0.001% to 12% per annum. The denominations ranged from $50 to $5,000. Most of the notes were one-year Interest Bearing notes. In later issues some were 60-day notes, one-year or two-year notes and were issued until 1861.

Since these notes carried interest and needed to be turned in to be redeemed, very few are to be found today.

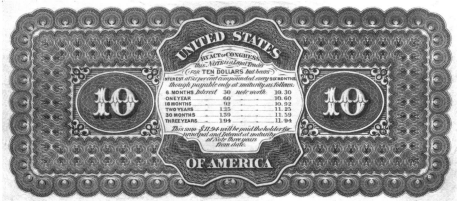

$10 Note, 1864, Compound Interest Treasury Notes. Portrait of Salmon Chase.

COMPOUND INTEREST TREASURY NOTES

Compound Interest Treasury Notes were issued by the Treasury Department in 1863 and in 1864, during the Civil War of 1861-1865, and were in general circulation. These notes were issued in denominations of $10, $20, $50, $100, $500 and $1,000 and were legal tender at face value. The compound interest was 6% per annum, payable only at the end of three years from the date of issue, printed in red on the notes.

A table of interest marking the exact value of the notes every six months was printed as part of the design on the back of all these notes. Thus, the $10 note was worth $10.30 after six months and $10.60 at the end of the first year. At the end of two years it was worth $11.25 and at the end of three years it was worth $11.94. All other denominations were calculated in a similar fashion.

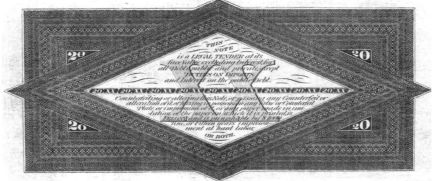

$20 Note, 1864, One Year, 5% Interest Bearing Notes. Portrait of Abraham Lincoln.

INTEREST BEARING NOTES OF THE CIVIL WAR 1861-1865

Four types of Civil War **Interest Bearing Notes** were issued during the Civil War years 1861-1865.

i. 60-day notes in denominations of $50, $100 and $500, with 5% interest per annum

ii. One-year Interest Bearing Notes issued in denominations of $10 to $5,000, with 5% interest per annum

iii. Two-year Interest Bearing Notes issued in denominations of $50 to $1,000, with 5% interest per annum

iv. Three-year Interest Bearing Notes issued in denominations of $50 to $5,000, with 7.3% interest per annum and redeemable at the end of three years. Five coupons were attached to each note, each redeemable separately every six months.

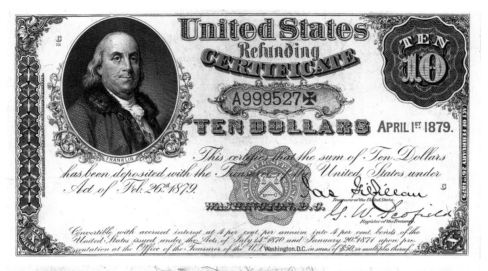

$10 Note, 1879, Refunding Certificates. Portrait of Benjamin Franklin.

REFUNDING CERTIFICATES OF 1879

Unlike the Interest Bearing Notes of the Civil War, **Refunding Certificates** were only issued in $10 notes in 1879 with 4% interest per annum. Originally they were issued with no time limit so the owners would hold onto them for as long as they could. Congress froze the interest on July 1, 1907, since they were accumulating large sums of interest. The value of the $10 note at the time of the freezing of the interest was $21.30.

$5 Note,
1861.
Portrait of
Alexander
Hamilton.

DEMAND NOTES 1861-1862

Demand **Notes** were issued from 1861-1862 - the Civil War years; some consider these to be the first circulated currency of the U.S. They were only printed as Large Size notes and were printed in black and green on the face and only green on the back. This is where the term **Greenbacks** for U.S. currency originated. They were called **Demand Notes,** however they were not redeemable in gold on demand but only at certain treasury offices.

They were printed in denominations of $5, $10 and $20.

■ On the face of the $5 note appeared

a portrait of Alexander Hamilton, first Secretary of the Treasury, and the Statue of Freedom, that stands on the top of the dome of the Capitol building in Washington D.C.

■ On the face of the $10 note appeared a portrait of Abraham Lincoln who was still alive when it was first issued, an eagle and an allegorical figure.

■ The face of the $20 note showed *Liberty* holding a sword and shield.

The back of all the notes carried a guilloche design with lettering and digits all in green.

$5 Note, 1864,
Confederate States
of Richmond.
Portrait of
C.G. Memminger.

CONFEDERATE CURRENCY 1861-1865

Confederate Currency was created by the Confederate States of America. In 1860, following Abraham Lincoln's election to the Presidency, eleven states broke away from the Union to create the Confederate States of America. This was the root cause of the Civil War of 1861-1865.

During the years 1861-1865, the Confederate States issued their own currency in several variations and denominations ranging from 50 cents to $1,000. They depicted portraits of famous Confederate leaders and vignettes of different topics, such as significant Confederate landmarks or scenes of the Civil War. They were first issued as one-sided notes, however later issues were printed on both sides of the paper and some bore interest.

At the end of the Civil War in 1865, all the states re-united and the Confederate currency was by then worthless and no longer in use.

The 11 Confederate States Of America

- South Carolina
- Mississippi
- Florida
- Alabama
- Georgia
- Louisiana
- Texas
- Virginia
- Arkansas
- North Carolina
- Tennessee

50 Cents Note,
1875.
Portrait of
Abraham Lincoln.

5

FRACTIONAL CURRENCY 1863-1876

Fractional Currency was first issued during the years of the Civil War, 1861–1865. People preferred metal money – coins – over paper money, as did the banks. For this reason banks avoided giving out change in coins preferring to hold on to them, which encouraged the public to do the same. As a result there was no small change in circulation in the form of silver or gold coins and people had to accept goods in their place. This situation was intolerable and the Treasury had no choice but to issue the **Fractional Currency** for the public to use as small change.

The name **Fractional Currency** derives from the fact that they were a fraction of the whole, the dollar, they were in values of cents, not dollars. The denominations were 3, 5, 10, 15, 25 and 50 cents. There were five different series issued during the years 1862-1876 and each denomination was printed in many varieties of size and color combinations. They all carried a portrait on the face and an abstract design on the back. They resembled miniature banknotes.

$10 Note, 1896, Large Size. Portrait of Daniel Webster; presentation of the Indian Princess Pocahontas to the British royal court on the right.

This note is one of the **Rainbow Notes**, a unique series of the United States Notes - Legal Tender, issued only in 1869. Due to the many colors used in the printing, they were called the **Rainbow Notes.** They were issued in all the denominations from $1 to $1,000. No other United States Notes - Legal Tender, issued either before or after, were as colorful as this series.

UNITED STATES NOTES – LEGAL TENDER 1862-1994

United States Notes, also referred to as Legal Tender Notes, were printed as Large Size and Small Size Notes. They were first issued in 1862 in denominations of $1, $2, $5, $10, $20, $50, $100, $500, $1,000 $5,000 and $10,000.

On the face they carried portraits of prominent people of the U.S., such as politicians, generals and statesmen, together with other elements, such as illustrations of statues, animals, or vignettes on various topics.

On the back of all the notes were abstract designs – guilloches – and text, with three exceptions. The back of the $5,000 and the $10,000 notes series of 1878 depicted an eagle above a shield and a U.S. flag. The $10 note series of 1901 depicted *Columbia* standing between two columns.

In 1869, a colorful version of these notes was issued. It is called the **Rainbow series**.

A unique note in this category is the $10 note of 1901 depicting the two famous explorers, Meriwether Lewis and William Clark, not politicians, generals or statesmen but still privileged to appear on a note. Furthermore, this note is the only one to have a mammal – a buffalo – as the central subject on the face of the note. This is why it was nicknamed "Buffalo Bill."

In 1928 the **United States Notes Legal Tender** were redesigned using the same design as the **Federal Reserve Bank Notes** issued at the time, but they were inscribed **United States Notes.** The redesigned $1, $2, $5, and $100 notes were issued until the 1960s, when they were gradually withdrawn from circulation. (See p.90.)

$10 Note, 1901, Large Size. Bison between the portraits of Lewis & Clark.

$5 Note, 1929, Large Size, National Currency. Portrait of Abraham Lincoln.

NATIONAL CURRENCY

1863-1938

National Currency notes were printed as Large Size Notes and Small Size Notes. They were issued from 1863-1938. This was the most complex system of issuing notes and had thousands of versions. Adding to this already complicated system was the fact that there were three Charter periods.

Charters were agreements between the Treasury and privately-owned banks, permitting them to issue banknotes. The Charters were limited to a 20-year period and then had to be renewed.

There were 14,320 national banks that issued notes and each had to deposit bonds at the Treasury as security to back the notes they issued. Each bank was limited to issuing up to 90% of the value of the bonds they deposited in the Treasury.

In order to simplify this complicated system, the Treasury retained the same basic design on the face of all notes for each denomination of each Charter period and only minor changes were made to the design.

The only significant difference was that the name of the issuing bank and the bank charter number were printed in large letters on the face of the note.

- The **First Charter Period** was from 1863-1902 and the notes were issued in one series.

- The **Second Charter Period** was from 1882-1922 and the notes were issued in three different series.

- The **Third Charter Period** was from 1902-1929 and the notes were issued in three different series.

When these notes were first issued they were accepted at less than their face value, depending on which bank had issued the note. The more trusted banknotes were accepted at a higher value. As confidence in the **National Bank** system grew, this practice was dispensed with and the notes were all accepted at their face value.

$10 Note, 1929, Large Size, National Currency. Portrait of Alexander Hamilton.

$10 Note, 1863. The First Charter Period.

The First Charter Period notes do not have portraits on either the face or back, but vignettes of important events, allegorical figures or landmarks in the history of the United States of America.

The landing of the pilgrims is depicted on the back of the $1 note issued in 1863 and 1875.

Christopher Columbus sighting land and the presentation of an Indian Princess are depicted on the face of the $5 note issued in 1863 and 1875.

The Committee of Five presenting the draft of the Declaration of Independence to Congress is depicted on the back of the $100 note issued in 1863 and 1875.

The illustration of the Committee of Five is based on John Trumbull's painting which hangs in the U.S. Capitol building. A century years later, this same illustration was selected to appear on the back of the $2 note issued to commemorate the Bicentennial of the Independence of the United States of America in 1976.

$10 Note, 1882, Second Charter Period, first issue.

The Second Charter Period of the National Currency Notes was from 1882 to 1902. These notes were issued in three different series, in denominations of $5, $10, $20, $50, and $100.

The design on the face of all denominations - with the exception of the $5 note – were identical to the design on the notes of the First Charter period for all three issues.

The $5 note was redesigned and portrayed President James Garfield who had been assassinated in 1881.

The design on the back of these notes was different for each of the three series, as shown below.

In the first series, the design and illustrations on the back were printed in brown. The Charter Number of each issuing bank was printed in the center in large digits, surrounded by guilloches.

In the second series, the back was redesigned and printed in green. The years, 1882-1908, were printed across the center in large digits.

In the third series, the design was almost identical to the previous one, however the denomination replaced the calendar year of the previous series.

$100 Note, 1902, Third Charter Period, second issue. Portrait of John J. Knox.

The Third Charter Period of the National Currency Notes was from 1902-1922. It, too, was divided into three issues. All the notes were redesigned but each denomination was identical throughout all three issues. This time portraits of prominent people of the United States appeared on the face; the back of each denomination illustrated a different topic.

Nevertheless, in order to differentiate between the three issues, the following differences were made in the designs.

In the first series, a red seal was printed on the face; no year was printed on the back.

In the second series, a blue seal was printed on the face; the years 1902-1908 were printed on the back.

In the third series, a blue seal was printed on the face; no year was printed on the back.

In 1929, these notes were redesigned, printed in Small Size format and last issued in 1935.

$20 note, 1882, Large Size, Gold Certificate. Portrait of James Garfield.

8

GOLD CERTIFICATES 1865-1936

Gold **Certificates** were issued initially for the same reason the Fractional Currency had been issued two years earlier – the public had more confidence in metal currency than paper currency. In order to gain the public's trust in these notes, they were issued as Gold Certificates and were redeemable for gold on demand.

Gold Certificates were first issued in 1865 and printed in Large Size format. They were printed using orange as the primary color so that they could be easily differentiated from the notes already in circulation.

Gold Certificates were in denomina-

tions of $10, $20, $50, $100, $500, $1,000, $5,000 and $10,000, though not all denominations were issued simultaneously. Most of these issues were circulated to the public, but the higher denominations were mainly used in the banks and clearing houses. The law for redeeming notes for gold was altered from time to time. Some notes were redeemable by banks and some only by the U.S. Treasury.

The notes were later redesigned, printed in Small Size format and issued from 1928-1934. They were then withdrawn from circulation and are no longer in use today.

$5 Note, 1870, Gold Bank Note.

THE NATIONAL GOLD BANKS

The notes of the **National Gold Banks** were unique and were only printed as Large Size notes. Nine California banks and one Boston bank issued these notes during the years 1870-1875. **Gold Banks** were national banks authorized by Congress also as Gold Banks. The California gold rush was the main reason for issuing of these notes. It was to provide an easy and efficient means of trading gold in the form of paper rather than the cumbersome gold metal.

They were printed on orange paper in order to give the impression of gold and to differentiate them from other currency in circulation at the same time. Another distinctive difference was the design on the back. The frame was similar to that of the national notes already in circulation, but in place of an illustration in the center there was a photograph of gold coins of all denominations. These are the only U.S. currency notes that have a photograph printed on them rather than an illustration. It is unusual and possibly unique.

$10 note, 1908, Large Size, Silver Certificate. Portrait of Thomas Hendricks.

Silver Certificates 1878-1965

Silver Certificates were issued in **Large Size Notes** and **Small Size Notes** and were legal tender. They were issued in denominations ranging from $1 to $1,000 in five different issues between 1878-1923. These notes also carried portraits of prominent U.S. personalities, such as Union Generals, Secretaries of the Treasury and former Presidents. The Silver Certificate notes also depicted allegorical figures, such as the eagle, and the head of an Indian chief known as **Ta-to-ka-in-yan-ka** – the Running Antelope – a member of the Sioux Indian tribe.

The most beautiful notes of the Silver Certificate type were the three issued in 1896, due to the elaborately illustrated subject printed on the face. These notes were issued to emphasize the achievements of the United States over its 120 years of existence.

For this reason, this series of notes is known as the **Educational Notes**.

Silver Certificates were redesigned and re-issued in several different versions at various times. They were last issued in 1963 and then gradually withdrawn from circulation.

The first of the Educational Notes was the $1 note, showing the Constitution, a woman pointing to the Potomac River, a young boy, the Washington Monument and the Capitol. The names of great Americans appear in the design of the frame of the note. George and Martha Washington appear on the back of the notes.

The second is the $2 note, depicting a group of five figures and elements representing science and electricity.

The third is the $5 note, with allegorical figures of women and the Capitol in Washington D.C. in the background.

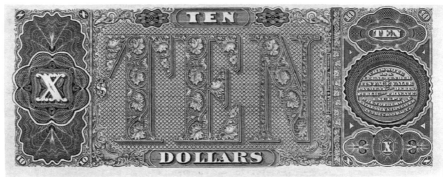

$10 note, 1890, Large Size, Treasury Note. Portrait of Philip H. Sheridan.

TREASURY NOTES – COIN NOTES

1890-1899

Treasury Notes – Coin Notes were only printed in Large Size format. They were issued from 1890 to 1899 in denominations of $1, $2, $5, $10, $20, $50, $100 and $1,000. They were inscribed **Treasury Notes** and were made of paper, but specified that they were **Dollars in Coins**, which meant they were redeemable as metal coins of gold or silver on demand. The decision as to whether they would be redeemed in gold or silver was left to the Secretary of the Treasury. The notes were backed by metal reserves of silver purchased by the Treasury. They, too, carried portraits of Union Generals and prominent U.S. personalities, such as Edwin M. Stanton, Secretary of War, and John Marshall, the fourth Chief Justice of the U.S. Supreme Court.

$10 Note, 1914, Large Size, Federal Reserve Note. Portrait of Andrew Jackson.

FEDERAL RESERVE NOTES
1914 TO THE PRESENT DAY

The Federal Reserve System was established in 1913 and is the system still in use today.

The country was divided into twelve districts. A Federal Reserve Bank was established for each district and one of its responsibilities was to issue and handle the notes for its district.

In order to make it easier to identify which banks issued which notes, each bank was assigned a letter and its equivalent number which were printed on each note.

The use of the notes was not restricted to the districts in which they were issued and they were accepted country-wide. They are still accepted world-wide.

The notes are inscribed **Federal Reserve Note** as they are issued by the **Federal Reserve System**, not by the **Federal Reserve Banks**. They were different from the **Federal Reserve Bank Note** (p.90) which was issued by the **Federal Reserve Banks** at the same time.

The twelve banks are: **A-1** Boston; **B-2** New York; **C-3** Philadelphia; **D-4** Cleveland; **E-5** Richmond; **F-6** Atlanta; **G-7** Chicago; **H-8** St. Louis; **I-9** Minneapolis; **J-10** Kansas City; **K-11** Dallas; **L-12** San Francisco.

Under the newly-established system all the notes were printed only by the Bureau of Engraving and Printing, commonly referred to as the B.E.P.

Federal Reserve Notes were first printed in **Large Size** format and issued in 1914 in denominations of $5, $10, $20, $50, and $100. The higher denominations of $500, $1,000, $5,000 and $10,000 were first issued in 1918. All the notes have a portrait and a circular design with the name of the issuing bank and its assigned number and letter on the face. The Treasury Seal is printed in red or blue on the right.

The following illustrations appear on the back of the notes.

5 DOLLARS
Back: Columbus sighting land and the landing of the pilgrims
Face: a portrait of Abraham Lincoln

10 DOLLARS
Back: farmers at work and factories
Face: a portrait of Andrew Jackson

20 DOLLARS
Back: a car, train and an airplane, a large ship and small boat, the Statue of Liberty, buildings in the background
Face: a portrait of Grover Cleveland

50 DOLLARS
Back: an allegorical figure of Panama on a background of land and sea with a ship on either side
Face: a portrait of Ulysses S. Grant

100 DOLLARS

Back: allegorical figures
Face: a portrait of Benjamin Franklin

500 DOLLARS

Back: the discovery of the Mississippi
River by De Soto
Face: a portrait of John Marshall

1,000 DOLLARS

Back: an eagle poised on a U.S. flag,
olive branches and arrows
Face: a portrait of Alexander
Hamilton

5,000 DOLLARS

Back: George Washington resigning
his commission
Face: a portrait of James Madison

10,000 DOLLARS

Back: embarkation of the pilgrims
Face: a portrait of Salmon Chase

In 1928, all these notes were redesigned and printed in Small Size format. The denominations of $5, $10, $20, $50 and $100 are still in use today, though most have been redesigned at least twice since they were originally issued.

$2 note, 1914, Large Size, National Currency, Federal Reserve Bank Note.
Portrait of Thomas Jefferson.

12

FEDERAL RESERVE BANK NOTES 1915-1945

Federal Reserve Bank Notes were only intended for temporary use. With the creation of the Federal Reserve System in 1913, **Federal Reserve Notes** (p.87) were issued to replace the **National Currency** bank notes (p.77) in circulation.

Issuing **Federal Reserve Bank Notes** at the same time as the **Federal Reserve Notes** was done to avoid the possibility of a shortage of money supplies during the transition from the National Currency system of banknotes to the newly established Federal Reserve System and Notes.

Federal **Reserve Bank Notes** were first issued in 1915 in Large Size format and were also inscribed **National Currency**. They were completely different from the National Currency that was already in circulation issued, by privately-owned banks.

The first issue, in 1915, consisted of three denominations: $5, $10 and $20. The second issue, in 1918, consisted of six denominations: $1, $2, $5, $10, $20 and $50.

The portraits were printed on the left of all the notes, the name of the issuing Federal Reserve Bank in large letters in the center and the Treasury Seal on the right.

On the back of the notes were illustrations of allegorical figures, or an eagle, ships, trains or significant events relating to the history of the United States.

In 1929, all the notes were redesigned and printed in Small Size format with a portrait in the center, the name of the issuing Federal Reserve Bank on the left and the Treasury Seal on the right in red. The assigned letter of the Federal Reserve Bank was printed four times on the face of each note and as a prefix letter to the serial number of the note.

They were last issued in 1945 and then gradually withdrawn from circulation.

$10 note, 1929, Small Size, National Currency, Federal Reserve Bank Note.
Portrait of Alexander Hamilton.

$1 Note, Silver Certificate, HAWAII overprint. Portrait of George Washington.

13

EMERGENCY NOTES WORLD WAR II

After the attack on Pearl Harbor in 1941, during World War II, emergency notes were issued for use by the U.S. Armed Forces.

Hawaii emergency notes were in fact the **Silver Certificates** or **Federal Reserve Notes** already in use at that time but with two additions: HAWAII was overprinted on them twice, once in small font on the face and then in a large outlined font across the back.

Silver Certificates were used in Europe and North Africa and they,

too, were altered and printed with a yellow seal on the face, as opposed to the blue seal printed on all the other notes in circulation at that time.

After World War II, from 1946 until the early 1970s, Military Payment Certificates were issued for the use of U.S. military and certain civilian personnel in the various occupied areas and military bases. They do not resemble any U.S. notes in circulation today.

$\mathcal{P}$art 3

High Denomination Notes

The $500, $1,000, $5,000 and $10,000 notes are High Denomination Notes first issued by the **Treasury of the United States** as early as 1861. Later on they were issued by the **Federal Reserve Bank** and were in circulation until 1969. They were last printed in 1945, but withdrawn from circulation in 1969 because people were not using them. However, they are still redeemable at face value at Federal Reserve Banks. Collectors will pay more than face value for them.

The notes presented in the following pages are the Small Size **High Denomination Notes** issued by the **Federal Reserve Bank.** They were issued in two series: the first in 1928; the second in 1934.

FIVE HUNDRED DOLLARS

b. January 17, 1706
d. April 17, 1790

William McKinley Jr. appears on the face of the note.

An abstract design appears on the back of the note.

WILLIAM McKINLEY JR. was the twenty-fifth President of the United States, serving from 1897 to 1901.

Born in Niles, Ohio, on January 29, 1843, he was the seventh of nine children.

He enlisted in the Union Army at the start of the American Civil War in June 1861. After the war he studied law and was admitted to the bar in 1867. He practiced law in Canton, Ohio.

McKinley was elected president in 1897 and promised to promote industry and banking. He led the country in the 100-day War - the Spanish-American War - bringing Guam, the Philippines, Cuba and Puerto Rico, formerly Spanish colonies, under American control.

William McKinley was the first President to have his inauguration filmed.

On September 6, 1901, an assassination attempt on McKinley took place at the Pan-American Exposition in Buffalo, New York. He was shot twice by Leon Czolgosz. One bullet was easily located and extracted, but doctors were unable to find the second; it was feared that the search for the bullet, might cause more harm than good. Since McKinley appeared to be recovering well, the doctors decided to leave the bullet where it was.

He survived for just over a week but then died from gangrene on September 14, 1901. He was buried in Canton, Ohio.

A five-hundred dollar note with the portrait of William McKinley Jr. on the face;
a guilloche design, with wording and digits in green on the back.

William McKinley appeared on the $10 notes
of the National Currency period.

**One of the many statements attributed
to McKinley is:**

*"In the time of darkest defeat, victory
may be nearest."*

ONE THOUSAND DOLLARS

b. March 18, 1837

d. June 24, 1908

Grover Cleveland appears on the face of the note.

An abstract design appears on the back of the note.

STEPHEN GROVER CLEVELAND was both the twenty-second (1885–1889) and the twenty-fourth (1893–1897) President of the United States, the only one to be elected to a second term which did not run consecutively with the first.

Cleveland was born in Caldwell, New Jersey, on March 18, 1837, the fifth of nine children. Age sixteen at the time of his father's death, Cleveland had to forego his dreams of college and help support his family. He worked with his older brother in New York City and was a part-time law student in Buffalo. Although he never attended college, he was admitted to the bar in 1858 at the age of 22.

In 1881, he was elected mayor of Buffalo. In 1882 he was elected Governor of New York. In 1884, he was elected President of the United States. In 1885, he ordered the military campaign against the southwestern Apache tribe led by Chief Geronimo, who was captured in 1886.

Grover Cleveland is the only America president to marry in the White House (June 1886). He was against the right of women to vote. In October 1886 the Statue of Liberty was inaugurated after President Grover Cleveland accepted it on behalf of the United States. He retired to Princeton, New Jersey, and died of a heart attack in 1908 at the age of 71.

Cleveland's portrait first appeared on the $1,000 note of 1907 and on the first few issues of the $20 Federal Reserve notes of 1914. He also appeared on the $1,000 note from 1928 to 1946.

A one-thousand dollar note with the portrait of Grover Cleveland on the face;
a guilloche design, with wording and digits in green on the back.

**Two of the many statements attributed
to Cleveland are:**

*"Though the people support the government,
the government should not support the people."*

■

*"The United States is not a nation to which
peace is a necessity."*

FIVE THOUSAND DOLLARS

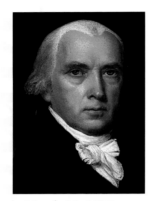

b. March 16, 1751
d. June 28, 1836

James Madison appears on the face of the note.

An abstract design appears on the back of the note.

JAMES MADISON was the fourth President of the United States of America, serving from 1809 to 1817.

He was born in 1751 and grew up as the oldest of twelve children, of whom nine survived.

He was one of the most influential of the founding fathers of the United States and is known as the Father of the Constitution and the Father of the Bill of Rights.

As President, Madison led the nation in the War of 1812, against Britain. During the war the British won numerous victories and occupied Washington D.C., forcing Madison to flee the city as the White House was set on fire by the British troops. During and after the war, Madison reversed many of his viewpoints and by 1815, he supported a national bank, a strong military, and a moderate tax structure.

When he left office in 1817, he retired to Montpelier, his tobacco plantation in Virginia. He left the presidency a poorer man than when he entered, due to the financial collapse of his plantation. He died at Montpellier on June 28, 1836. He was 85 years old and the last surviving signatory of the United States Constitution.

James Madison appeared on the 1878, $5,000 United States Note and on a $100 and $5,000 Gold Certificate note.

A five-thousand dollar note with the portrait of James Madison on the face;
a guilloche design with wording and digits in green on the back.

**Two of the many statements attributed
to Madison are:**

*"A man has a property in his opinions and
the free communication of them."*

■

*"Philosophy is common sense
with big words."*

TEN THOUSAND DOLLARS

b. January 13, 1808
d. May 7, 1873

Salmon Portland Chase appears on the face of the note.

An abstract design appears on the back of the note.

SALMON PORTLAND CHASE was an American politician and jurist during the Civil War era.

Chase was born in Cornish, New Hampshire. He studied law and was admitted to the bar in 1829. In 1855 he was elected Governor of Ohio. He became Secretary of the Treasury under Abraham Lincoln in 1861.

As Secretary of the Treasury from 1861 to 1864, during the years of the Civil War, two major changes in American financial policy took place. The first was the establishment of a national banking system which he favored. The second was the issue of legal tender, the greatest financial blunder of the war, and carried out contrary to his recommendation.

In 1864 he was appointed Chief Justice of the United States, a position which he held until his death in 1873. Chase died in New York City and was buried in the Oak Hill Cemetery in Washington, D.C. He was later re-interred in the Spring Grove Cemetery, in Cincinnati, Ohio.

In an effort to promote his political career, his own portrait appeared on various U.S. banknotes, unheard of today but acceptable then. Thus he appeared on the $1 United States Legal Tender Notes and the $10 Compound Interest Treasury Notes of the Civil War.

In honor of the fact that he introduced the modern system of banknotes, Chase later appeared on the $10,000 note, printed from 1918 to 1946. It is no longer in circulation.

A ten-thousand dollar note with the portrait of Salmon Chase on the face;
a guilloche design, with wording and digits in green on the back.

The Chase National Bank, a predecessor of the
Chase Manhattan Bank, was named in his honor,
though he had no financial affiliation with it.

**One of the many statements attributed
to Chase is:**

"The way to resumption is to resume."

ONE HUNDRED THOUSAND DOLLARS

b. December 28, 1856
d. February 3, 1924

Woodrow Wilson appears on the face of this Gold Certificate.

An abstract design appears on the back of the note.

The Four U.S. Presidents Awarded the Nobel Peace Prize

- Theodore Roosevelt (1905)
- Woodrow Wilson (1919)
- Jimmy Carter, Jr. (2002)
- Barack Obama (2009)

WOODROW WILSON was the twenty-eighth President of the United States of America, serving from 1913 to 1921.

He was born in Virginia in 1856. A graduate of Princeton University (then the College of New Jersey) and the University of Virginia Law School. He also held a doctorate from Johns Hopkins University.

Wilson served two terms as President and regarded himself as the personal representative of the people. "No-one but the President," he said, "seems to be expected... to look out for the general interests of the country."

The creation of the **Federal Reserve system** was one the major pieces of legislation passed during his presidency, as well as the law that prohibited child labor and the limiting of the work load of railroad workers to an eight-hour day.

On May 9, 1914, President Wilson proclaimed the first U.S. **National Mother's Day** to be celebrated as a day for American citizens to fly the flag in honor of those mothers whose sons had died in war.

In 1917 Wilson declared America's entrance into World War I as a crusade to make the world "safe for democracy." In 1919 President Wilson was awarded the Nobel Peace Prize and is one of only four American Presidents to be awarded the honor.

Wilson died at his home on February 3, 1924. He is the only President buried in Washington, D.C.

*A one-hundred thousand dollar note with the portrait of Woodrow Wilson on the face; a guilloche design, with wording and digits in red on the back.

Woodrow Wilson is the only person to appear
on the $100,000 note.

**Two of the many statements attributed
to Wilson are:**

"Caution is the confidential agent of selfishness."

■

"Tell me what is right and I will fight for it."

∗ This note was a **Gold Certificate** not issued to the general public but intended only for the use of banks and clearing houses. This is the largest denomination issued in the United States of America.

INDEX

Portraits of people whose names appear in **bold** in the index below appear on notes.

ILLUSTRATIONS

BIBLIOGRAPHY AND FURTHER READING

- **Currency Notes** – The Bureau of Engraving and Printing, Washington.
- **Official Blackbook Price Guide to United States Paper Money.** Crown Publishing Group, New York.
- **Standard Catalog of World Paper Money, General Issues 1650-1960.** Edited by Neil Shafer and George S, Cuhaj. Krause Publications, Iola, 2003.
- **Standard Catalog of World Paper Money, Modern Issues 1961-Date.** Edited by Neil Shafer and George S, Cuhaj. Krause Publications, Iola, 2003.
- **The World Almanac and Book of Facts.** 140th Anniversary Edition. World Almanac Books, New York, 2008.
- **Time Almanac 2008.** Encyclopedia Britannica, New York, 2008.
- **Paper Money of the United States,** by Arthur L. Friedberg and Ira S. Friedberg. 19th edition. The Coin and Currency Institute Inc., Vermont.

BANKNOTE ILLUSTRATIONS

Courtesy of:

Heritage Auctions, pages 67, 75

Coin & Currency Institute, page 67

National Numismatic Collection, Smithsonian Institution, page 103

Federal Reserve Bank of San Francisco, pages 88, 89

Elon Malis

Romano House of Stamps

Author's collection